GW00537641

Jazz Ballads

16 Famous Jazz Ballads
16 bekannte Jazz Balladen

Arranged by / arrangiert von:
Dirko Juchem

Piano Score / Klaviersatz:
Harald Rutar

ED 21179
ISMN 979-0-001-17848-8
ISBN 978-3-7957-4582-0

Flute
Flöte

Mainz · London · Berlin · Madrid · New York · Paris · Prague · Tokyo · Toronto
© 2011 SCHOTT MUSIC GmbH & Co. KG, Mainz · Printed in Germany

Contents / Inhalt

The CD was recorded and mastered at / die CD wurde aufgenommen & gemastert bei
Pauler Acoustics, Northeim

The musicians playing on this CD are / die Musiker auf der CD sind:
Dirko Juchem – Flute / Flöte
Harald Rutar – Piano / Klavier
Manfred Hilgers – Double Bass / Kontrabass
Bruce Busch – Drums / Schlagzeug

About The Songs

The selection of titles in this volume comprises songs with interesting histories that illustrate the origins of the musical energy and magic in jazz: I'd like to tell those stories here.

Night And Day

Cole Porter composed this song in 1931 for his musical "Gay Divorce". Fred Astaire sang this jazz classic both in the musical and in the 1934 film of (almost) the same name, "The Gay Divorcee". There are numerous versions of this song: probably the best known are those by Ella Fitzgerald, Frank Sinatra and Bing Crosby, along with the more recent recording by Rod Stewart.

Strangers In The Night

Originally, Bert Kaempfert composed this melancholy evergreen under the title "Beddy Bye" for a adventure comedy film – "A Man Could Get Killed"(1966). In the same year, "Strangers In The Night" was the title song of Frank Sinatras most successful record and made him win several Grammys in 1967. Sinatras extraordinaire scat improvisation of the melody actually inspired the cartoon canine Scooby Doo.

Moon River

...is indisputably one of the most beautiful love songs in film history.
This song won the Oscar for the best song written for a film in 1962, when it featured as a love song in the film "Breakfast At Tiffany's".
Audrey Hepburn sang the song in the film, but there have been many fine versions by other singers such as Paul Anka, Louis Armstrong, Barbara Streisand, Frank Sinatra and many more...

Blue Moon

Richard Rodgers and Lorenz Hart worked together for many years and composed many of the great jazz classics. In the 1920s they collaborated on numerous Broadway musicals and from the 1930s onwards they also worked in the emerging film industry in Hollywood.
Blue Moon is one of the greatest hits by these two exceptional composers.
The song has been sung by celebrated jazz musicians including Ella Fitzgerald, Frank Sinatra and Dean Martin – and later on by Elvis Presley, too, and many others.

Über die Songs

Die Titelauswahl dieses Bandes beinhaltet Songs mit bemerkenswerten Entstehungsgeschichten, welche die Herkunft der musikalischen Energie und Magie des Jazz erläutern und die ich euch hier darstellen möchte.

Night And Day

Cole Porter hat dieses Lied 1931 für sein Musical „Gay Divorce" komponiert.
Fred Astaire sang diesen Jazzklassiker sowohl in dem Musical, als auch in der (fast) gleichnamigen Verfilmung „Gay Divorcée" von 1934. Es gibt zahlreiche Versionen von diesem Song, die wohl bekanntesten stammen von Ella Fitzgerald, Frank Sinatra und Bing Crosby, sowie in neuerer Zeit von Rod Stewart.

Strangers In The Night

Ursprünglich komponierte Bert Kaempfert diesen melancholischen Evergreen unter dem Namen "Beddy Bye" für eine Abenteurkomödie – "A Man Could Get Killed" (1966).
Im gleichen Jahr war „Strangers In The Night" der Titelsong von Frank Sinatras erfolgreichstem Album, das ihn mehrere Grammys gewinnen ließ. Sinatras außergewöhnliche Scat-Improvisation über die Melodie war Inspiration für den Cartoon-Hund „Scooby Doo".

Moon River

...ist unbestreitbar eins der schönsten Liebeslieder der Filmgeschichte!
Als Liebesballade in dem Film „Frühstück bei Tiffany" erhielt dieser Song 1962 den Oscar für den besten Film-Song.
Der Song wurde im Film von Audrey Hepburn gesungen, es gibt aber auch viele wunderschöne Versionen von anderen Sängern, wie Paul Anka, Louis Armstrong, Barbara Streisand, Frank Sinatra und vielen anderen...

Blue Moon

Richard Rodgers und Lorenz Hart arbeiteten über viele Jahre zusammen und haben zahlreiche der ganz großen Jazz-Klassiker komponiert. In den 20er Jahren haben sie für zahlreiche Broadway Musicals gearbeitet und ab den 30er Jahren auch für die aufkommende Filmindustrie in Hollywood.
Blue Moon ist einer der größten Hits dieser beiden Ausnahmekomponisten. Gesungen wurde der Song von bekannten Jazzmusikern – unter anderem von Elly Fitzgerald, Frank Sinatra und Dean Martin - aber später auch von Elvis Presley und vielen anderen!

Wayfaring Stranger

This traditional gospel song has been equally popular with jazz and folk musicians. Famous vocal recordings have been made by the folk singer Emmy-Lou Harris and by Eva Cassidy.

The version presented here tends more towards the phrasing of the jazz flautist Jeremy Steig, who recorded this song for his Blue Note album of the same name.

Frankie & Johnny

This traditional folk song is about the dramatic end of a love affair: Johnny leaves Frankie, who is overcome by jealousy and shoots him dead.

Many celebrated musicians have performed this song, including Louis Armstrong, Johnny Cash, Duke Ellington and Stevie Wonder. The song also inspired the film of the same name starring Elvis Presley.

Fly Me To The Moon

This song was originally written in ¾ time with the title "In Other Words". Frank Sinatra recorded this jazz classic in 1964 with the Count Basie Big Band, launching one of his greatest hits ever. That recording of "Fly Me To The Moon" was played by the crew of the spaceship Apollo 10 during their orbit of the moon, when it was broadcast on television all over the world.

Autumn Leaves

With words by Jacques Prévert, Joseph Kosma's song "Les feuilles mortes" first became known as a French chanson. In the English version with words by Johnny Mercer "Autumn Leaves" became one of the major jazz classics of all time.

There are famous versions by Doris Day, Frank Sinatra, Marlene Dietrich, Miles Davis, Stan Getz, Keith Jarrett, Eva Cassidy and many more...

As Time Goes By

This jazz ballad became world famous in 1942 through the film "Casablanca", of course – although it was composed by Herman Hupfeld back in 1931.

Dooley Wilson, who sings the song in the film, was actually a jazz drummer and only sat behind the piano for the role of the bar piano player Sam in Rick's "Café Américain".

Wayfaring Stranger

Dieser traditionelle Gospelsong wurde von Jazz- und Folkmusikern gleichermaßen gerne interpretiert. Berühmte gesungene Versionen gibt es von der Folksängerin Emmy-Lou Harris und von Eva Cassidy.

Die hier vorliegende Version orientiert sich eher an der Phrasierung des Jazzflötisten Jeremy Steig der diesen Song für sein gleichnamiges „Blue Note" - Album aufnahm.

Frankie & Johnny

In diesem traditionellen Folksong geht es um das dramatische Ende der Liebesbeziehung von Johnny, der sich von seiner Frankie abwendet, die ihn daraufhin aus Eifersucht erschießt.

Viele berühmte Musiker haben diesen Song interpretiert, darunter Louis Armstrong, Johnny Cash, Duke Ellington und Stevie Wonder. Das Lied war auch Vorlage für den gleichnamigen Film mit Elvis Presley.

Fly Me To The Moon

Dieser Song wurde ursprünglich im Dreivierteltakt und unter dem Titel „In Other Words" komponiert. Im Jahr 1964 nahm Frank Sinatra diesen Jazzklassiker gemeinsam mit der Count Basie-Bigband auf und landete damit einen seiner ganz großen Erfolge. Genau diese Aufnahme von „Fly Me To The Moon" wurde von der Besatzung des Raumschiffs Apollo 10 während ihrer Mondumrundung abgespielt und ging während der Fernsehübertragung um die ganze Welt.

Autumn Leaves

Mit einem Text von Jaques Prévert wurde „Les feuilles mortes" von Joseph Kosma zunächst einmal als französischer Chanson bekannt. In der englischen Version, mit einem Text von Johnny Mercer, wurde „Autumn Leaves" zu einem der bedeutend-sten Jazzklassiker aller Zeiten.

Berühmte Versionen stammen von Doris Day, Frank Sinatra, Marlene Dietrich, Miles Davis, Stan Getz, Keith Jarrett, Eva Cassidy und vielen mehr...

As Time Goes By

Weltbekannt wurde diese Jazzballade natürlich durch den Film „Cassablanca". Im Jahr 1942 - obwohl sie schon 1931 von Herman Hupfeld komponiert wurde.

Dooley Wilson, der diesen Song im Film singt, ist eigentlich Jazzdrummer und setzte sich nur für die Rolle des Barpianisten Sam in Ricks „Café Américain" hinter das Klavier.

Amazing Grace

In this song John Newton tells of his conversion to Christianity. In the 18th Century Newton was the captain of a slave ship that was almost lost in a storm at sea. In desperation he prayed to God, and after he was saved he began to treat the slaves with more consideration, later giving up his trade altogether to become a preacher.

Take The A-Train

The "A-Train" is line A on the New York subway, the route that links Brooklyn with Manhattan and Harlem. This jazz classic became the signature tune of the Duke Ellington Band and Ella Fitzgerald also used the "A-Train" as the opening song at many of her concerts.

Wade In The Water

As one of the best-known American spirituals this song belongs to the standard repertoire of every gospel choir, though it has also been sung by many well-known jazz, soul and pop musicians.
Some of the most popular versions are by Ramsey Lewis, the Golden Gate Quartet, the Harlem Gospel Singers and more recently the singer Eva Cassidy.

Petite Fleur

The soprano saxophonist and clarinettist Sidney Bechet had his greatest hit with this instrumental number, selling over ten million records.
Bechet, who was born in New Orleans, lived in Paris for many years and was revered there as "le Dieu" ("God"). Although he never really learned to read music, he is one of the most influential performers to have come out of New Orleans jazz and was known particularly for his rich vibrato sound.

Satin Doll

Duke Ellington may properly be called one of the most important jazz composers. Ellington composed his famous "Satin Doll" in 1958. This song is particularly notable for the inspired sequence of typical jazz chords (II – V and II – V – I progressions).

Amazing Grace

In diesem Lied erzählt John Newton von seiner Bekehrung zum Christentum. Newton war im 18ten Jahrhundert Kapitän eines Sklavenschiffes, das in schwere Seenot geriet. In seiner Not betete er zu Gott und nach seiner Errettung behandelte er zunächst die Sklaven mit mehr Menschlichkeit, später gab er seinen Beruf sogar ganz auf und wurde Prediger.

Take The A-Train

Der „A-Train" ist die Linie A der New Yorker U-Bahn, die Brooklyn mit Manhattan und Harlem verbindet.
Dieser Jazzklassiker wurde zum Erkennungslied der Duke Ellington Band und auch Ella Fitzgerald hat den A-Train in vielen ihrer Konzerte als Eröffnungssong benutzt.

Wade In The Water

Als einer der bekanntesten amerikanischen Spirituals gehört dieser Song zum Standardrepertoire eines jeden Gospelchores, wurde aber auch von vielen bekannten Jazz- Soul und Popmusikern gesungen.
Einige der populärsten Versionen stammen von Ramsey Lewis, dem Golden Gate Quartet, den Harlem Gospel Singers und aus neuerer Zeit von der Sängerin Eva Cassidy.

Petite Fleur

Mit diesem Instrumentalhit hatte der Sopransaxophonist und Klarinettist Sidney Bechet mit mehr als 10 Millionen Schallplatten seinen größten Erfolg.
Bechet, der in New Orleans geboren wurde, lebte viele Jahre in Paris und wurde dort als „le Dieu" („Gott") verehrt. Obwohl er nie richtig Noten lesen konnte, gehört er zu den wichtigsten Solisten des New Orleans - Jazz und war besonders für seinen an Vibrato reichen Sound bekannt.

Satin Doll

Duke Ellington darf zu Recht als einer der bedeutendsten Komponisten des Jazz bezeichnet werden.
Sein berühmtes „Satin Doll" hat Ellington 1958 komponiert. In diesem Song fällt besonders die geniale Folge der für den Jazz typischen Akkordwendungen (den II - V, bzw. II - V - I - Verbindungen) auf.

How High The Moon

This song comes from the 1940s musical "Two For The Show", but thanks to its unusual and complex chord structure it very quickly became one of the most popular titles in bebop music.

Ella Fitzgerald's version of the song, with her spectacular vocal scat interludes, became especially famous. In those days it was common practice for musicians to compose new melodies to go with popular songs in the jam sessions that were very popular at the time. Not every player would always be able to identify the underlying song straight away, which was meant to deter less talented musicians from participating in these jam sessions. Charlie Parker composed his famous "Ornithology" to the harmonies of "How High The Moon".

My Way

Paul Anka wrote the English lyrics to the French chanson "Comme d'habitude" by Claude François and Jacques Revaux. Paul Anka himself said that he wrote the words for Frank Sinatra, who went on to have a worldwide hit with this lovely song. The lyrics tell of a man who has travelled the world in his lifetime and finally looks back over it all.

Have fun with these "Jazz Ballads"!
Best wishes, Dirko Juchem

How High The Moon

Dieser Song stammt aus dem 40er Jahre Musical „Two For The Show", wurde aber aufgrund seiner ungewöhnlichen und komplexen Akkordstruktur sehr schnell zu einer der beliebtesten Titel im Bebop.

Besonders berühmt wurde die Version von Ella Fitzgerald, mit ihrer für die damalige Zeit spektakulären Scat-Gesangseinlage. Zu dieser Zeit war es allgemein üblich, zu populären Songs neue Melodien zu komponieren, damit bei den damals sehr beliebten Jam Sessions nicht jeder Musiker den eigentlichen Song sofort erkennen konnte. Hiermit sollten die weniger guten Musiker gehindert werden, an den Jam Sessions teilzunehmen. Auf diese Weise komponierte Charlie Parker zu den Harmonien von „How High The Moon" sein berühmtes „Ornithology".

My Way

Paul Anka schrieb den englischen Text zu dem französischen Chanson „Comme habitude" von Claude Francois und Jacques Revaux. Nach eigener Aussage hat Paul Anka den Text ganz gezielt auf Frank Sinatra zugeschnitten, der mit diesem wunderschönen Song dann auch einen Welthit gelandet hat. In dem Text geht es um einen Mann, der in seinem Leben um die Welt gekommen ist und am Schluß nochmal eine Rückschau auf sein Leben hält.

Nun aber VIEL SPASS mit den „Jazz Ballads"!
Euer Dirko Juchem

Night And Day

Musik und Text: Cole Porter
Arrangement: Dirko Juchem

54 464

33 | F#m7b5 ... Fm7 ... Em7 ... Ebo

roa - rin traf-fic´s boom, or__ in the si - lence of my lone - ly__ room I

37 | Dm7 ... G7 ... Cmaj7 ... Bb7

think of you_____ day and night._____ Night and

Swing (ternär)

B

41 | Ebmaj7 ... Cmaj7

day, un - der the hide of me,_____ there's an

45 | Ebmaj7 ... Cmaj7

oh, such a hun - gry yearn - ing__ burning in - side of me And it's

Bossa Nova

49 | F#m7b5 ... Fm7 ... Em7 ... Ebo

tor - ment won't be through_____ `til you let me spend my life__ mak - in' love_ to you

53 | Dm7 ... G7 ... C ... Bb7#11

day and night,_____ night and day.__ night and day_

57 | C ... Bb7 ... C ... Bb7 ... C

__ day__ and__ night night and day

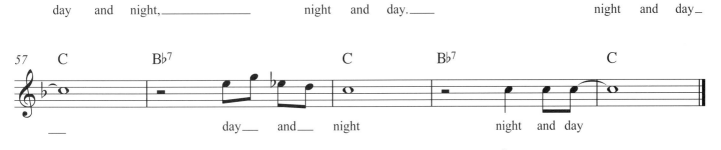

rit. _ _ _ _ _ _

54 464

Strangers In The Night

Musik: Bert Kaempfert
Text: C. Singleton und E. Snyder
Arrangement: Dirko Juchem

Strangers in the night exchanging glances
Wond'ring in the night what were the chances
We'd be sharing love before the night was through

Something in your eyes was so inviting
Something in your smile was so exciting
Something in my heart told me I must have you

Strangers in the night
Two lonely people, we were strangers in the night
Up to the moment when we said our first hello little did we know
Love was just a glance away, a warm embracing dance away
and

Ever since that night we've been together
Lovers at first sight, in love forever
It turned out so right for strangers in the night

Love was just a glance away, a warm embracing dance away
Ever since that night we've been together
Lovers at first sight, in love forever
It turned out so right for strangers in the night

Moon River

Musik: Henry Mancini
Text: Johnny Mercer
Arrangement: Dirko Juchem

54 464

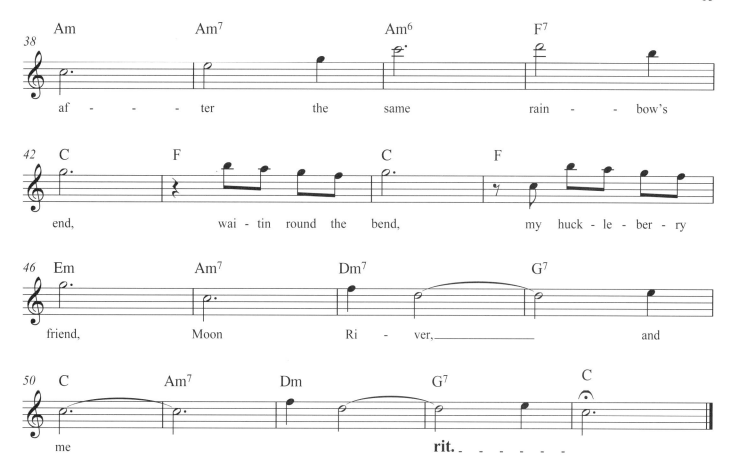

af - - ter the same rain - - bow's

end, wai - tin round the bend, my huck - le - ber - ry

friend, Moon Ri - ver, _____ and

me

rit. _ _ _ _ _ _

Henry Mancini

Blue Moon

Musik: Richard Rodgers
Text: Lorenz Hart
Arrangement: Dirko Juchem

54 464

Wayfaring Stranger
aus Amerika

Traditional
Arrangement: Dirko Juchem

Frankie & Johnny

Traditional
Arrangement: Dirko Juchem

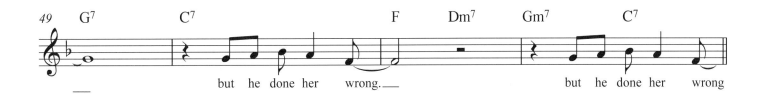

Fly Me To The Moon
(In Other Words)

Musik und Text: Bart Howard
Arrangement: Dirko Juchem

Rechte für Deutschland, Österreich, Schweiz, Griechenland, Türkei und Osteuropa
ESSEX MUSIKVERTRIEB GMBH, Hamburg.   54 464

23

54 464

Autumn Leaves
(Les feuilles mortes)

Musik: Joseph Kosma
Originaltext: Jacques Prévert
Engl. Text: Johnny Mercer
Arrangement: Dirko Juchem

As Time Goes By

Musik und Text: Herman Hupfeld
Arrangement: Dirko Juchem

54 464

Amazing Grace
aus Schottland

Traditional
Arrangement: Dirko Juchem

54 464

Take The A-Train

Musik und Text: Billy Strayhorn
Arrangement: Dirko Juchem

54 464

Solo - A1

Hur - ry,___ get on___ now it's co - ming.

List - en,___ to these___ rails a - hum - ming;_____ all a -

board_____ get___ on the A - Train._____ Soon___

You will be on su - gar hill in Har - lem.

Wade In The Water

Traditional
Arrangement: Dirko Juchem

Ramsey Lewis

Petite Fleur

Musik: Sidney Bechet
Text: Sidney Bechet und Ferdinand Bonifay
Arrangement: Dirko Juchem

D **Swing**

E **Tango**

Sidney Bechet

Satin Doll

Musik: Duke Ellington und Billy Strayhorn
Text: Johnny Mercer
Arrangement: Dirko Juchem

54 464

How High The Moon

Musik: Morgan Lewis
Text: Nancy Hamilton
Arrangement: Dirko Juchem

54 464

My Way
Comme D'Habitude

Musik: Jacques Revaux und Claude François
Originaltext: Gilles Thibaut
Engl. Text: Paul Anka
Arrangement: Dirko Juchem

54 464

times, I'm sure you knew_____ when I bit off_____ more than I could chew. But through it all,_____ when there was doubt,_____ I ate it up_____ and spit it out. I faced it all_____ and I stood tall,_____ I did it my_____ way. I did it my_____ way

rit. _ _ _ _ _ _ _ _

Frank Sinatra